HEROES IN TIME OF WAR

Famous
American
Heroes
and Leaders Series:

Founders of Fortunes, Book One

Founders of Fortunes, Book Two

Founders of Our Cities

Citizens Born Abroad

Explorers of Our Land

Heroes in Time of War

Famous American Women

HEROES
IN TIME
OF WAR

by

L. EDMOND LEIPOLD, Ph.D.

Publishers

T. S. DENISON & COMPANY, INC.

Minneapolis

DEDICATION

To my son
DAREL JOHN

Foreword

Times of war and other national crises have a tendency to bring forth leaders who rise to the occasion and provide the leadership necessary to take their nation through the period of danger to the new era that lies ahead.

The men whose interesting life stories are told in this book are excellent examples of such leaders. Sometimes their contributions have been brief ones, while in other cases the periods of service have extended into years. The courageous father who bade his son good-bye from the roadside is nameless, but his words have lived through the decades that have since passed. All of them have, through word or deed—or both—left messages that have served to inspire countless persons.

Perhaps in this book their life stories will inspire many others who might not otherwise come to know of the contributions that they have made to our valorous history.

L.E.L.

Contents

General George Amstrong Custer

Destiny on the Little Big Horn

More has been written about the battle of the Little Big Horn River than about any other battle in American history. It was a small skirmish, as battles go, for there were only a few more than two hundred soldiers—and a few civilians—killed in the battle. There were no wounded; only the dead. In countless other battles during our national history there were more casualties by far, and the names of the conflicts are no longer even remembered, but every American knows of the fight on the Little Big Horn River in Montana.

What is known of the battle must be deduced from the scene that met the eyes of fellow soldiers who came looking for Custer and his men, for there were no survivors and only the enemy saw the fight, and they were loathe to tell about it.

There was something very strange about the battle. There are things that to this day are still unexplained, though the battle took place in June of 1876. Indians traditionally hit and ran. After inflicting heavy losses on their foe, they faded into the hills before their own losses became too great. But at the Big Horn, they hit and hit again; they continued striking until there were no more of the white soldiers left.

Why their tactics were different on this occasion can only be guessed at. They hated "Yellow Hair" with a deep and intense hatred, for hadn't he killed their women and children early one morning as they came out of their lodges, with their warrior men away in the hills and no one there to protect them? "Woman fighter" they called him, and they hated his long yellow hair that fell in folds onto his shoulders. It was his pride, but an insult to the Indians, for didn't most white men cut their hair short to make scalping less easy if the fight went wrong? Was it fate that caused Custer on the eve of his departure on his last campaign to cut his hair short at last?

There had been great excitement in the Indian camp the evening before the battle, for a group of the boys—no one knew how many— had formed a suicide squad and had taken the oath to die in the next battle. The boys who had taken the death vow had withdrawn from the camp. Then when the excitement was at its peak, they had made a dramatic entrance. Wild cheers greeted them; some of the Indians began a death chant; others formed a ring around the central camp- fire and began a stomping, frantic war dance. Yellow Hair would suffer on the morrow if he were brash enough to come near them; this was their promise. There was Cut Belly, only seventeen years old, and Little Whirlwind, who had already proved his valor in battle, and Noisy Walking and Closed Hand, and others. They would all die the next day, just as their white foes would.

What manner of man was this long-haired soldier who was so hated by the Indians? Was he a brave man? Everyone agrees that he was. Was he a wise general? Here they hesitate. He had on other occasions shown wisdom, but on this fatal occasion he divided his troops into three groups and went confidently looking for the enemy with only a third of his fighting force with him. True, he underesti- mated the strength of the Indians ahead—but would a wise general have made this error? And true, too, he disregarded warnings of his scouts about the size of the Indian force that was somewhere ahead in the hills and for whom he was searching. Would a wise general have done this?

That Custer had a purpose in what he did, we must accept with- out question. Was he so confident of victory, whatever the odds may have been, that overconfidence clouded his judgment? If he was, the error was a fatal one. Once the enemy appeared, there was no opportunity to revise his judgment, or to retreat and regroup and try again. The die had been cast; fate now controlled the tide of battle, and the Indians had planned well. Custer and his men were fighting to save their lives; the Indians fought with a deep hatred that gave them strength even beyond their needs, for they outnumbered their foe by ten to one.

General George Armstrong Custer is as controversial a figure today as he was on that day in June of 1876 when at noon he started up the Rosebud with some six hundred soldiers, forty-six Indian scouts of the Arikara and Crow tribes, some twenty civilian guides and packers, and one newspaper correspondent promising to send a lively report to his newspaper back East. Among the soldiers was Custer's younger brother, a favorite of his.

George Armstrong Custer was born in Ohio on December 5, 1839. His father was a blacksmith and a farmer. His paternal great-grandfather was a Hessian soldier in Burgoyne's army during the American Revolution who, after the surrender of Burgoyne, went to Pennsylvania, where he settled down. George's ambition as a boy was to be a soldier and he was fortunate in being appointed to West Point by his local congressman, there to receive his military training.

At West Point he was not a good student and neglected his studies to such an extent that when he graduated four years later he was at the foot of his class. He served in various capacities during the Civil War, and after being cited for gallant conduct at Aldie, he was given the rank of brigadier general. His energy and dash won him wide acclaim and soon he was one of the most celebrated commanders in the Union Army. He pursued the Confederate General Lee relentlessly, and when the surrender of Lee came, Union General Sheridan said, "I know of no one whose efforts have contributed more to this happy result than those of Custer."

With the fighting ended, Custer was transferred to the Southwest with the rank of Lieutenant Colonel in charge of the 7th Cavalry, remaining with it until his death on the Little Big Horn. He took part in several Indian campaigns, becoming a controversial figure involved in an unsuccessful campaign in 1867 in which it appears that he was made the scapegoat. He was court-martialed and sentenced to a year's suspension from the Army. Upon his recall he rejoined his regiment and won a victory over the Cheyennes at Washita under Black Kettle.

In 1875 he led an expedition through the Black Hills on orders from the War Department to investigate reports that white men were filtering into the Hills in search of gold, though a treaty with the Indians had set that region aside to be forever Indian territory. His journey apparently served to spread the rumors, and the influx of adventurous men into the area led indirectly to the fatal campaign of the next year.

In March of 1876, General Custer was summoned to Washington to testify before a Congressional committee concerning alleged frauds and irregularities in the Indian Service. The testimony that he gave was viewed by President Grant with great disfavor and he stripped him of his command and forbade him to return to the West to take part in the proposed campaign against the rebellious tribes. So great was the storm of popular disapproval, however, that Grant relented and Custer rejoined his regiment, ready to begin the three-pronged campaign which had been planned the year before.

As he began his last march, resentment filled General Custer's mind. He felt that he had been treated unfairly, and to a proud man, such feelings become broodings. That he wanted to regain the esteem which he felt had to some degree been taken from him is very probable. He was a man of integrity, and he felt that his testimony in Washington was honest and to the best interests of the Indian Service. However, he had been humiliated instead of respected, and his resentment was deep.

Such were his feelings as he prepared to play his part in the campaign which, it was hoped, would destroy forever the fighting power of the Indians in that region.

The plan to force the errant tribes back on their reservations was a simple one. The attacking forces of our soldiers were three in number; one unit led by the experienced old Indian fighter, General George Crook. The second unit, led by Colonel John Gibbon, had just come from western Montana; the third, containing the forces of General George Custer, had come westward from the Missouri River. They had met where the Rosebud flows into the Yellowstone, there to plan the final campaign.

Crook's unit, however, had failed the rendezvous, for when penetrating into Montana the week before, he had met the combined forces of the Sioux and had come out second best in the encounter. This the soldiers at the mouth of the Rosebud did not know. Meanwhile, the Indians, having tasted victory, were eager for another battle, their numbers justifying their confidence.

Meanwhile, Gibbon prepared to move up the Yellowstone River to the Big Horn, then follow that stream south to the Little Big Horn. Custer was to go south along the Rosebud, paralleling Gibbon's route, thus hemming the Indians between them. Then Custer was to move across from the Rosebud, meeting Gibbon at the Little Big Horn, where they would jointly prepare to attack. With these plans in mind, the units separated and Custer moved up the Rosebud with his men on June 22 at high noon.

Meanwhile, unknown to Custer, the Indians, fresh from their encounter with Crook, had set up camp on the Little Big Horn. There were perhaps ten thousand of them, including three thousand warriors eager for battle. The Sioux included Sitting Bull's Hunkpapas and many Oglalas; there were also some Arapahoes and Northern Cheyennes. Altogether, they were a formidable fighting force.

As Custer came up the Rosebud he was informed by his scouts that the foe that he was searching for was west of him on the Little Big Horn, and without waiting for Gibbon, he set out alone, prepared to do battle. What impelled him to do this will never be known, for certainly he knew the danger of it. Did he want the honor alone and not share it with Gibbon? Did he plan to recoup his military fortunes by making a master stroke all by himself? Some have said that he remembered "The Pathfinder" Fremont, who was rewarded for his exploits by being nominated for the Presidency. Whatever his motives were, he forsook the agreed upon plan and set out alone to seek the hostile tribes.

Arriving at the Little Big Horn he failed to see the huge Indian camp, hidden well by trees. The last decision in his fatal plan sealed his doom. Now he divided his men into four groups: one was to remain with the slowly moving supply train to guard it; the second unit, under Captain Benteen, was to move to the southwest to prevent the escape of the Indians in that direction; the third, under Major Reno, was to attack the Indian camp at its southern end; the fourth, with Custer in charge, moved to attack at the northern end of the camp. Such was the plan—but plans can go wrong.

Reno carried out his part of the campaign, but the unexpectedly large force of Indians inflicted heavy losses on his men and they retreated to a protective bluff on the Little Big Horn, across from the Indian camp, where the pack train and Benteen's forces joined them in a battle that continued all night and through the next day. Heavy firing could be heard from Custer's direction on the second day, but there was no way of knowing what was going on there nor could help be sent. Then all was quiet and no more sound of gunshots was heard on the prairie.

The next day the remainder of the troops from the Yellowstone arrived and joined Reno and Benteen; together they moved toward the Indian camp in search of Custer. They found the camp deserted, the Indians having left the evening before. Custer, they assumed, was following them, so the group pushed on. Then they found them, at first one or two, then several, then Custer and the main force, all dead, many mutilated. The positions of the bodies told the whole story.

There had simply been too many of the foe for the two hundred men to oppose. And the Indian suicide squad, they were there too; they had died like heroes as had those who opposed them. Never had there been such a battle; never would there be one like it again.

Today many questions continue to be asked: Why did Custer move against the Indians alone without waiting for Gibbon's unit, as had been agreed upon? Why, when battle was imminent, did he make the tragic mistake of dividing his forces still further?

Someone has quoted Custer as once saying, "My Seventh Cavalry can outfight any group of hostiles of any size anywhere." Was this confidence in his men the cause of his overplaying his hand? We shall never know, for everyone who took part in the battle is now dead. Only the Indians lived into the day following the battle, and they told little. It was enough for them to know that "Long Hair" was dead, punished for what they felt were his wicked deeds. But we, of his same race, honor him for the gallant battle that he fought on the banks of the Little Big Horn River on the lonesome Montana prairie on June 26, 1876.

Dwight David Eisenhower

Soldier and President

The average American boy, it is said, dreams of the day when he will be President of the United States. Whether Dwight Eisenhower ever had such dreams he has not said, but he probably never thought, when he was going to school in Abilene, Kansas, that he would someday be commander of the Allied Armies in Europe, united in their attempt to crush a cruel enemy, and then return home to be twice elected President of our country. That, in brief, is his life story.

Texas can claim the honor of being the birthplace of Dwight Eisenhower, for he was born in the town of Denison, Texas, on October 14, 1890. His grandfather was a pioneer who went to the prairie state of Kansas when it was still largely unsettled and there became a farmer, preaching on Sundays in the community church. His ancestors had come to America about the time that George Washington was a boy, settling in Pennsylvania. Though they were Germans, they became known as "Pennsylvania Dutch," an honest, hard-working group that still has extensive and prosperous farms west of Philadelphia.

The family name was then spelled "Eisenhauer," which, translated, means "Hewer of iron." We would call such a person a blacksmith or simply a smith. Many names can be traced back in this way to the occupation of the person named.

Dwight's father became owner of some of his own father's rich Kansas farmlands, but he did not like farming and sold his land, becoming a storekeeper. In this business he was not successful and he decided to go to Texas, where he also failed to make a living as a businessman. It was while the family lived in Denison, Texas, that their son, whom they named Dwight David, was born.

Disappointed in being unable to make a success of his business venture, the father once again decided to move, returning to Abilene, Kansas, when Dwight was two years old. Although money was scarce, his mother resolved that her children should have the best education possible, and credit must be given to her for keeping her boys in school.

Good marks came easy for Dwight during his high school years and he enjoyed his studies. He was a good athlete, taking part in all of the athletics that he could. After he finished high school he was unable to decide for some time just what he wanted most to do, at one time seemingly quite determined to go adventuring in South America, but those plans were short-lived due to lack of money.

He took a job in a local creamery, working long hours for small pay. Dissatisfied with his work, he decided to make application for entrance to either the army school at West Point, New York, or the naval academy at Annapolis, Maryland. His reasoning was that if he wasn't accepted at one of the schools, he might be at the other. Surely two chances were better than one, he thought.

"Ike," as he was known to his friends, was pleased to learn that he placed first in the naval academy's examination and second in the West Point test. It looked as if he were about to become a naval officer trainee when he learned that he would be too old to meet their age requirements by the time he could enroll there. Then a fortunate thing happened: the young man who placed first in the West Point entrance test was unable to accept the appointment, so Ike was chosen in his stead. He entered West Point in the summer of 1911, beginning an army career that was to take him to the very top of his profession as a soldier.

Strangely enough, his parents, like his grandparents before them, were pacifists; that is, they did not believe in war; so it was regarded by some people as unusual that the son should be training for a fighting career. However, his parents did not oppose him in his choice of careers and Dwight went ahead with his plans to be a professional soldier.

Four years later he graduated from West Point in the top half of his class, and as a Second Lieutenant, was assigned to duty at Fort Sam Houston, Texas. Here he met the lovely Mamie Dowd, daughter of a wealthy Denver family, whom he married. Two children were born to them, one of whom died when three years old; the other, John, like his father, chose to make army life his career.

Lieutenant Eisenhower's next twenty years were much like those of other men who went to West Point to become professional soldiers. He became a major, remaining at that rank for sixteen years. Selected by the Operations Chief, Major Connor, to assist him in the War Department, Eisenhower made a fine success of it and was chosen to take further training in the General Staff School. There were two hundred and seventy-five enrolled; Ike placed first, at the head of the class.

Such a promising officer was not neglected by the higher army officials. He was selected to attend Army War College in Washington; he next studied at the Industrial War College, then went to Europe to examine battlefields there. He was made Assistant Executive Officer in the office of the Secretary of War, his immediate superior being General Douglas MacArthur, who was at that time the Army Chief of Staff. General MacArthur was sent to the Philippines as military adviser and Eisenhower went along as his assistant, where he remained for four years.

He was given the position of Chief of Staff of the Third Army, and when extensive training maneuvers were held, the Third Army "defeated" its opponent, and Eisenhower was given credit for planning the successful campaign. His reputation was excellent, for he had shown that his long years of training had taught him well the fundamentals of warfare.

The "day of infamy" arrived, December 7, 1941, when the Japanese struck Pearl Harbor, our naval base in the Hawaiian Islands, without warning. Our Pacific fleet was crippled, the base was in ruins, thousands of our armed forces were dead or injured. Again we were at war.

Eisenhower was ordered to report to Washington at once to help in planning the strategy that the United States would use against the Japanese who at the moment were victorious in many operations. The Philippines were under attack and would soon fall. It seemed as if nothing could stop the Japanese, for they were fanning out in all directions in the Pacific area. British strongholds, too, were falling one by one; even Australia seemed in danger.

When Eisenhower's opinion was sought on the tactics to be used to stop the Japanese and to recover the lands already lost, he submitted a plan which General Marshall, who was in command, found to his liking and it became the strategy that proved to be so successful in our war against the Japanese, leading finally to the total collapse of Japan and its dream of controlling the entire Pacific area.

Shortly after he was called to Washington, Eisenhower was made head of the War Plans Division. His next assignment sent him to Europe to work with the British in their efforts to protect their own nation against invasion by the Germans and to free those nations already overrun by Hitler and his troops. He returned to Washington with a plan to unite the troops of the nations warring against the German armies, and soon his plan was approved by the American high command.

It was no surprise to most people when General Eisenhower was put in command of our troops in Europe, nor when he was made Commander General of all Allied troops. His task was to destroy the German military machine which had so far been invincible. Wherever the Germans attacked they were victorious. Poland, Austria, Czechoslovakia to the east were overrun; Belgium, Holland, Norway, Luxembourg, Denmark on the west all fell before Hitler's "blitzkrieg" or "lightning war." England came under heavy and almost constant attack from the air; how long it could hold out no one knew. Under Winston Churchill's inspiring leadership their morale remained high even as their cities were destroyed from the air. Somehow the English people remained sure that they would someday win the struggle.

In June of 1944, the day of decision arrived and all was in readiness; the continent of Europe was about to be invaded by the Allied troops composed of Americans, British, and fighting forces of many other nations. Hitler had boasted that his armies would never be defeated; no one knew how strongly defended the coast was. There was no way to find out but to try. A tremendous invading force had been assembled on the coast of England; its landing place was to be Normandy, across the channel on the French coast. There were ships of all kinds, large and small; there were planes to support the ground troops; food and supplies had to be right at hand at all times; ammunition for every kind of gun used was necessary. If a shortage developed in any essential item, the success of the invasion might be threatened. If the attempt should fail, another might not be made for years; still worse, perhaps it could never be made again.

General Eisenhower's invasion succeeded and soon our troops were spreading out over Western Europe. France was liberated; Belgium, Holland, the Scandinavian countries, were cleared of German troops. He hammered from the west while the Russians attacked from the east. Berlin fell, and Hitler, who had boasted that his empire would last for a thousand years, killed himself in his bunker far below the ground, even as his capital city of Berlin burned overhead.

The most terrible war in the world's history was over; millions had died, countless other millions had suffered fates worse than death; heroes were numerous, but the man honored by everyone was Dwight Eisenhower, supreme commander of the Allied Armies.

He returned to America, the nation's favorite hero. A great honor was extended to him when he was offered the position of President of Columbia University, one of America's greatest universities. Later he was Commander of the Allied Powers in Europe and was instrumental in organizing the North Atlantic Treaty Organization (NATO) for the defense of the Western World against Communism.

Many persons pleaded with him to run for the highest office that the American people can offer to any citizen, that of President of the United States. Yielding to their pleas, he resigned from the Army and accepted the Republican nomination. In the November election he overwhelmed his opponent, so popular was he with the American people. He had promised during the campaign that if he were elected President, he would seek means to end the Korean War in which our soldiers were engaged. He kept his promise, and to the relief of our nation, the war in Korea came to an end. When his first term of office was over he was re-elected for another four-year term.

President Eisenhower had had a long and distinguished career as soldier and President. Now he looked forward to retirement. He bought a farm on the outskirts of Gettysburg in Pennsylvania, scene of one of the Civil War's greatest battles, and there he retired to live as an elder statesman and to write his memoirs.

Presidents who followed him in the White House continued to seek his advice for they knew that his honorable record had given him experiences such as few men ever had. In retirement, as in active life, he had the respect and confidence of his fellow Americans.

Nathan Hale

One of America's Great Patriots

Times of war produce heroes, for it is when danger threatens that bravery often is at its best. The War of the Revolution, which gave us our freedom from England, also gave us many heroes, both men and women. As time passes, the names of many of these heroes are forgotten, to be found only in history books or in records filed away in some storeroom. There are some names, however, which will live in the memory of our nation as long as there is an America. Nathan Hale is one of these names.

The fighting had begun in the spring of the year 1775 when British troops closed the port of Boston to shipping to punish the people of that city for daring to defy the king. For one thing, they had dumped a shipload of tea into the harbor because the king demanded that it be permitted to be taken ashore, but this the colonists refused, since they were expected to pay a tax on it and they said that the British government had no right to tax them.

Things went from bad to worse. The people of Boston resented very much having the red-coated British soldiers in their city, and they let everyone, including the king's governor, know it. The patriots of Boston organized into groups called "Sons of Freedom," and they kept close watch on the troops to find out what they intended to do next. When there was evidence of much troop movement about

the city one day, it was learned that the British were going to march
to the nearby town of Concord to capture some powder and other
supplies that were being stored there. At once the alarm went out:
"The British are coming!"

Two lanterns that were hung in the tower of the Old North
Church, built high on a hill in Boston, warned two riders, Paul Revere and William Dawes, that the British were ready to move across
the river. At once Revere and Dawes mounted their horses and gal-
loped toward Lexington and Concord to warn the people along the
way that the British troops were on the move. That day the war began. There was fighting at Lexington and again at Concord and a
heavy toll was taken by the colonists as they kept up a constant fire
of their guns on the British troops which were now retreating in dis-
order to Boston.

A stone at Lexington marks the spot where the first fighting of
the Revolution took place. On it is engraved the words that the leader
of the troops, Captain Parker, spoke to his men as the British approached: "Stand your ground. Don't fire unless fired upon. But if
they mean to have a war, let it begin here."

The war that began at Lexington, Massachusetts, that April day
in 1775 did not end until General Washington captured Cornwallis
at Yorktown in faraway Virginia, six and a half years later, to
the day.

Not long after the fighting had taken place at Lexington and
Concord, a great battle took place at Bunker Hill, across the river
from Boston. The colonial troops were finally driven from their positions when their ammunition gave out, but so bravely had they
fought against the experienced British troops that they felt sure they
could give a good account of themselves in any battle that now might
come.

Overlooking the city of Boston and its harbor was Dorchester
Heights. The colonials were driven from Bunker Hill, it was true,
but by fortifying Dorchester Heights they could in turn gain an advantage over the British and even drive them from the city. The
plan worked, just as they thought it would. The British ships were

forced to leave the harbor or be destroyed by the American cannons looking down on them, so they pulled up anchor and sailed out to a safe distance.

Now it was the British troops that were left in Boston who were in trouble, for there was no way in which food could be taken to them. The land route was cut off and now no ships could dock, either. The British General Howe had little choice; it was either get out of Boston at once or stay and starve. He chose to leave. The people of Boston were treated to the rare sight one morning of seeing the Redcoats boarding their ships that were tied up at the docks. They sailed away to Halifax, in Canada, where they were safe from the guns of Washington's army. The fighting at Boston had ended, and though the war dragged on for more than six years, the Bostonians heard no more sounds of gunfire. The scene of battle shifted to other locations and never returned to the neighborhood of Boston.

General Howe in Canada was now faced with the necessity of making new plans in order to end the rebellion in the colonies against his king. He had been driven out of Boston, but there were other large and important cities in the colonies that he could capture to make up for it.

While examining his maps, he became aware of the many rivers which flowed through the colonies to the ocean. General Howe knew that if he could get possession of some of these important rivers and of the cities that had grown up where the streams flowed into the ocean, he could divide the colonies, cutting them off from each other.

There were at least four rivers which he felt should be controlled by the British. Far to the south there was the Savannah River in the colony of Georgia. Control that river and the colony of Georgia would be effectively cut off from all the others. Between Maryland and Virginia flowed the Potomac River on whose banks stood stately Mount Vernon, George Washington's home. Control the Potomac River and the Northern colonials would be separated from their Southern brothers, which could go a long way toward winning the war.

Then there was Chesapeake Bay into which the Delaware River flowed. The important city of Philadelphia lay on its shores, and that city still had many Tories among its residents, people who supported the king rather than the patriot's cause. The capture of Philadelphia would be a bold stroke indeed.

Farther to the north flowed the Hudson River, at its mouth the thriving city of New York. By controlling the Hudson River, the rebellious New England states would be separated from the other colonies. That would be a serious blow to the colonist's cause, so serious, in fact, that perhaps this move should be the one taken first of all.

In Canada was the British General Burgoyne. He could come south through Lake Champlain, march overland a short distance to the Hudson River, then go south on the Hudson to New York City. Meanwhile, General Howe would sail for New York City, to unite there with Burgoyne. It was a simple plan and a good one, for if it succeeded it might well deal a tragic blow to the cause of independence.

With these plans in mind, General Howe and his army left Halifax and sailed south, straight for New York, the most important city in the American colonies.

General Washington had long wondered what the next move of the British would be, and he correctly believed that the capture of New York City would be their next objective. He therefore took his army to New York, and soon the two opposing forces were camped almost within sight of each other. General Clinton had joined General Howe and reinforcements had also arrived from England, so it was a strong army that faced Washington and his forces. Just how strong it was, Washington had no way of knowing, but he planned to find out.

General Washington took the problem to his trusted General Knowlton, commander of a light infantry division. There appeared no other way to get the desired information than to send a spy inside the British lines, dangerous as such a procedure would be. They needed someone who was brave enough to risk capture and death, but who was also intelligent enough to get the information that was needed.

At once a young officer named Nathan Hale offered his services. Although he was just twenty-one years old, he already held the rank of captain. A former schoolteacher, he had enlisted in Washington's army with the hope that he could be of help in his country's struggle for freedom. He now volunteered for the hazardous role of spy with that same hope.

Captain Hale left on his mission at once. Presenting himself as a local resident, he first went to Connecticut, then crossed over to Long Island, where the British army was camped at Brooklyn. He made his way there, spending several days inside the British lines, making drawings of positions and taking notes about the strength and nature of the forces. Completing his work, he returned to the north side of Long Island and there awaited an opportunity to return to the mainland.

After waiting for some time, he saw a boat approaching which he believed was manned by sympathizers of the patriot cause from Connecticut. This proved to be wrong, and on the boat was a relative of his who was a Tory. Nathan Hale was promptly captured and taken to General Howe's headquarters.

Hale did not attempt to save himself by denying that he was a spy. When he was questioned, he readily admitted his guilt, whereupon General Howe ordered him to be hanged the following morning.

Never did any man face death more bravely than did Nathan Hale. His request that a minister of the Gospel be permitted to be with him during his final hours was denied; his request for a copy of the Bible for a final prayer was similarly refused. A farewell letter to his mother was destroyed by the British, as were other letters that he wrote early that fateful morning. The reason for these acts of cruelty was given by the British provost marshal: "The rebels must not know that they had a man in their army who could die with such firmness."

As Captain Hale ascended the scaffold, just as the sun was rising in the east, he was asked if he had any final words to say. Without faltering or show of fear, he spoke the words that have inspired Americans ever since: "I only regret that I have but one life to lose for my country."

Brave, intelligent, with his whole adult life about to be denied him, he did not plead for mercy nor did he whimper or complain of his fate. His only regret was that he could die but once for his native country. Surely he was one of America's greatest patriots. Never did a soldier die more bravely.

Andrew Jackson

Orphan - - Hero - - President

When Andrew Jackson was a boy, the Revolutionary War was in progress. Andrew's sympathies were very favorable to the American cause and he resented greatly some of the British officers' attitudes, which were overbearing, to say the least. Few of the British believed that the ragged colonial soldiers could possibly defeat the seasoned troops from England.

One day when Andrew was a prisoner of the British, the boots of one of the officers became spattered with mud and Andrew was ordered to clean them. This he refused to do, and the officer repeated his order. Once more Andrew refused, this time angrily, for he was of Scotch-Irish descent and he had a very fiery temper. On this occasion his face became as red as his hair, as he turned to leave the room without obeying the officer's order.

Now it was the officer's turn to let his anger flare, and drawing his sword from its sheath, he slashed Andrew across the face with it, inflicting a wound that left a scar which he carried throughout his lifetime. Andrew never forgot the incident and it often reminded him that liberty is retained by a nation—or an individual—only at the price of some sacrifices.

Andrew Jackson, born of humble parents in the backwoods Waxhaw region of South Carolina, orphaned when he was fourteen, through sheer grit and force of character, became a great general, idol of the common people, and President of the United States.

Andrew was born on March 15, 1767, of parents who had come to America from North Ireland to seek a new way of life in Colonial America. Two years later, shortly before the birth of Andrew, the father died, leaving the mother to struggle alone to support the family. She gave up their home and went to live with relatives. Here Andrew grew into his teens, tall, thin, red-haired, with a fiery temper and a reckless disposition.

When the British approached and the men of the neighborhood banded together to do battle, Andrew and his brother, though hardly old enough to shoulder their muskets, joined with them, and at the battle of Hanging Rock were captured and imprisoned. Here they both contracted smallpox which left their faces pitted and scarred. It was here, too, that Andrew received the slash from the British officer's sword.

They were released in time, but the brother, who had been wounded, died shortly afterward of the effects of his imprisonment. The mother, hearing of the great need of nurses in Charlestown to take care of the sick and wounded, hastened to that city and there worked long hours aiding the suffering soldiers. The strain proved to be too great, for she caught "prison fever" and died, leaving Andrew an orphan. He was fourteen years old.

He was bewildered and uncertain about what to do. He first went to Charlestown to learn what he could about his mother's death, then returned to the backwoods. Next he tried schoolteaching, but finding it not to his liking, turned to the study of law. Securing a very good horse, he headed westward and was soon studying law at Salisbury, in North Carolina.

The wild life of the frontier appealed to his unbridled nature and he entered avidly into the boisterous life of the community, finding cock-fighting, horse racing, and carousing much to his liking. For two years this was the kind of life he led, learning little of law but much about life on the frontier. Then he packed his bags, mounted his horse, and headed westward once again, this time stopping at Jonesboro in Tennessee, his saddle adorned with a fine gun, pistols, saddle bags, and fox hounds, ready to take his place as a "gentleman" in the rough community.

When the first road leading to the new settlement of Nashville opened in the fall of 1788, young Jackson, now twenty-one years old, was among the first to travel over it. There he took room and board with the widow of Colonel John Donelson, founder of Nashville, finding agreeable company in the person of Mrs. Rachael Robards, also a roomer there. Their friendship developed and the husband divorced Rachael, jealous of the attentions that Andrew gave her.

Under the impression that the divorce decree had been granted, Andrew and Rachael were married, but later it became known that it was two years after their marriage before the divorce became final. The resulting scandal followed the couple for many years, causing Andrew to kill a man because of slanderous remarks made by him, and even entering prominently into the presidential election of Jackson forty years later. The two young people were passionately devoted to each other for the remainder of their lives.

It did not take long for the energetic young lawyer to make a name for himself, and he soon assumed a prominent place in the community, being appointed prosecuting attorney for the district the year after he came to Nashville.

The new region was rapidly filling with people, and it became a territory of the United States in 1790. William Blount became governor and Andrew Jackson, young, energetic, and ambitious, became a close friend of the new governor. Land was the commodity in greatest demand on the frontier and young Jackson speculated wildly in it, often buying and selling thousands of acres at a time. One of the tracts acquired he called the "Hermitage," several miles out of Nashville. Here he made a home for himself and Rachael for the remainder of their lives, developing the land into a great cotton plantation. Today the Hermitage is a national shrine, visited by thousands of people each year, and it is one of the best preserved of all the presidential homes.

Andrew Jackson was one of the delegates to the convention held in 1796 to frame a constitution for the new state of Tennessee, a recognition of the high regard in which he was held. Tennessee was entitled to one seat in the House of Representatives in Washington, and Jackson was elected without opposition to be that representative. Governor Blount became one of the state's Senators at the same time and it was largely due to his influence that Andrew Jackson was so signally honored. Later Blount was expelled from the Senate and Jackson was elected to take his place.

He continued actively in the affairs of the state and was appointed a superior judge for Tennessee, a position which he filled energetically if not brilliantly. Meanwhile, he planted cotton at the Hermitage, visited with his friends around town, and raced his horses whenever occasion arose. He was, in his own eyes and in the eyes of the people of Nashville, living the life of a "country gentleman," the kind of life which he liked very much indeed.

It was at this time that he fought his famous duel with Charles Dickenson because of a remark made by him about Jackson's wife, Rachael. Dickenson was killed and Jackson was severely wounded, but because Dickenson had many friends, Jackson's name was blackened by the affair.

Sent to subdue the hostile Creek Indians who had massacred the inhabitants of Fort Mims in the Mississippi Territory, Jackson overcame many difficulties arising from the wild nature of the region and defeated the Indians in the Battle of Horshoe Bend, elevating him to the position of a local hero. He was made a major general in the United States Army and was sent to defend New Orleans against the British who were marching on that city.

His troops were raw and unseasoned, but his fortified position was a strong one, for the British had to approach the city over a narrow neck of land. It was here that Jackson built strong breastworks from behind which his men mowed down the advancing enemy without mercy, resulting in a notorious victory for the Americans. Three times the British advanced, and three times they were sent reeling back, each time leaving a general dead on the field of battle. New Orleans was saved and Andrew Jackson was a national hero, suddenly elevated to a position of prominence by his dramatic victory.

Andrew Jackson was at this time forty-eight years of age and perhaps at the peak of his physical and mental powers. In appearance, he presented an impressive figure. He was tall, thin to the point of emaciation, with a rather long and narrow face, and his red hair was thick and hard to control. His temper was quick and often violent. His loyalty to his friends was without bounds, but his foes were hated with deep intensity. While he was strong willed and often acted on his own sentiments, he usually thought important matters over carefully before reaching a decision.

This was the man who was now a national hero, with many people speaking of him as possible presidential material. However, President Monroe was in the White House and he was scheduled for another four-year term; and, since he was a friend of Andrew Jackson's, that man had no intention of running against him in 1820. But there would be another presidential election in 1824 and that would be another matter.

An incident now occurred that was typical of the kind of action in which General Jackson was inclined to become involved. Florida at this time (1818) belonged to Spain, and the Seminole Indians of that region sometimes raided American settlements, then fled back across the border to safety. Jackson was sent down there with troops to see what could be done about this unpleasant condition.

As usual, his action was forthright and drastic. When the Seminoles fled before him and escaped into Florida, he did not let the fact that he had no right to go into Spanish territory with his troops stop him. He followed them across the boundary, captured Pensacola, and not only punished the marauding Indians, but hanged two Englishmen who had been stirring up the red men and inciting them to attack the Americans.

The incident brought us close to war with both England and

Spain, but the Washington administration backed his actions, largely because the sentiment of the people in the West was highly favorable to Jackson's course of action. As a result of the incident, the United States bought Florida from Spain, and Monroe appointed Jackson to be the first governor of the newly acquired territory. Thus his action in invading Florida was, to a large extent, vindicated, though the governorship meant so little to him that he resigned it a year later and returned to the Hermitage to once again live the life of a country gentleman.

With his usual ability to become easily involved in political affairs, he now permitted his name to be advanced as a presidential candidate in the forthcoming election of 1824, only two years away. A volunteer committee of friends worked hard to build Jackson up nationally as a "peoples" candidate and a friend of the "little" man. His military record was played upon heavily, especially the outstanding victory over the British at New Orleans and the punishing of the Florida Creeks.

In the midst of the campaign to popularize his name, he was appointed U. S. Senator from Tennessee in 1823, a position for which he had very little liking, holding it only long enough to pass it on to a friend.

In the presidential campaign, his opponents were Henry Clay and John Quincy Adams. Jackson received the largest number of peoples' votes, but neither candidate received enough electoral votes to be elected, so according to the Constitution it was now up to the House of Representatives to elect a president. The Clay forces gave their votes to Adams, who was declared elected. Unhappy about the outcome but unable to do anything about the matter but accept it, the Jackson campaign managers at once set about preparing for the election of 1828. It was still four years off, but they were planning carefully and well and did not intend to be defeated a second time.

Their success was little short of miraculous. During the four years Jackson was built up not only as a popular hero and military leader, but as a "man of the people." Everywhere he became known as "Old Hickory," the continuous campaign reaching a degree of enthusiasm never before realized. Jackson clubs were organized in every state, their sole object being the election of their favorite son to the presidency. Henry Clay's health forced him to retire from the race, further increasing Jackson's chances for success.

After the election was over and the votes were counted, Jackson was declared elected. His popular vote was four times as large as it was four years before. He carried all of the states of the West and South except Maryland. He even carried New York and Pennsylvania.

Jackson's inauguration on March 4 was an affair such as the capital city of Washington had never seen before. Thousands of people had come from all parts of the nation to see their hero take the oath of office as President of the United States. The slopes of Capitol Hill were covered by the eager populace, each one seeking a better position of vantage. A few minutes before twelve o'clock noon the presidential party emerged from the door of a hotel on the avenue, Jackson a head taller than most of the others, his shock of unruly white hair conspicuous above the rest of the party. They proceeded to the east portico of the Capitol where Chief Justice John Marshall administered the oath of office, after which the new President mounted his horse and rode to the White House, a mile down Pennsylvania Avenue, for the official reception.

The poor orphan boy of less happy days was now President of the United States.

The White House reception was a nightmare. The doors had been thrown open for all to attend—and apparently everyone did. The nation's most elegant society ladies were crowded elbow to elbow with scrub women; stable boys were for the moment socially equal to the wealthy gentlemen whose horses they curried earlier in the day. White people and black, rich and poor, young and old, each one crowded and jostled in an attempt to shake hands with Andrew Jackson. They rushed from room to room in the White House, they stood on chairs and even the tables; they upset trays of food and drink in the hands of servants. Jackson escaped out a side door, but the pandemonium inside continued. Finally a Solomon found a solution: the punch, so popular that day, was taken outside and served on the White House lawn; the crowd followed. All that the servants had to do now was to clean up the debris inside. Truly, Washington had never seen such a day—but then, there had never been a true "People's President" inaugurated before.

Andrew Jackson's eight years in the White House were as tumultuous as his previous life had been. There were few dull moments, for the differences that arose were sometimes as social as they were political.

One of Jackson's cabinet members married the daughter of a Washington tavern keeper, and it was widely rumored that her previous adventures had been many. Society women of the city sniffed, then snubbed her, thereby greatly offending Jackson, who took the matter personally. Martin Van Buren, another cabinet member and a bachelor, anxious to curry the favor of the President, was conspicuously agreeable to the lady, as he had no wife to deter him. Jackson noticed Van Buren's attentions and was greatly pleased. The two men became closer and closer friends, Van Buren eventually being selected to be the Vice President in 1832 and President in 1836.

The common people distrusted banks in general and the powerful U. S. Bank in particular. Jackson destroyed it by withdrawing government funds from it and depositing them in various state banks, thereby causing great distress among the monied class but greatly pleasing the much more numerous common people.

When the state of South Carolina threatened to refuse to obey a United States law that it disliked, Jackson vowed in turn that he would send troops there if necessary to enforce the law. At a Jefferson Day dinner he boldly offered the toast, "The Federal Union— it **must** be preserved!" thereby leaving no doubt in anyone's mind just where he stood.

Jackson was a strong-willed man and he did his duty as he thought that it should be done. When he was nominated for a second term, he received even more votes than he had received four years before.

At the end of eight years he gladly gave up the office of President to return once more to the Hermitage which he loved so well, but which for him was now a lonesome place, for his beloved wife Rachael had died. Here he lived quietly, interested in the affairs of the nation that he had served for so many years, but content to let others cope with its problems. With age his strength failed until in the early days of summer in the year 1845 he died, to be buried in the family plot at the Hermitage, to rest in death where he had lived with contentment during so many years of his life.

Captain James Lawrence

"Don't Give Up the Ship!"

The American Navy has had a long and honorable history, although it took many years for it to convince some of the nations that it would stand for no nonsense from them. During the American fight for freedom under General George Washington, we had no navy. France sent a fleet over to help us during the war, and it did a great service for our cause when it bottled up Cornwallis at Yorktown, preventing a British fleet from coming to the rescue of their trapped general.

This took place in the year 1781. Several years later a revolution took place in France, the king and queen were beheaded, and a different kind of government ruled the land. Because the United States had made a treaty with England in 1794 which the new French government did not like, the French became very angry and insulted our representative to the French court. Then they demanded that we pay them a large sum of money to keep their good will.

The American people and their government resented very much these actions by the once-friendly French and prepared for war. All over our country people were saying, "Millions for defense but not one cent for tribute!" Because it was expected that if war came it would be fought mainly on the sea, a Navy Department was created and a Secretary of the Navy was appointed to oversee the building of warships and the training of sailors to man the ships.

The Navy Department was created in the spring of the year 1798, and before the close of that year the United States had thirty-four ships of war out on the high seas searching for French vessels to destroy. Many were the battles fought and many were the victories won by our ships. It did not take long before the French had had enough of it and soon they let us know that they were ready for peace. We had let the world know that we were not a weak little frontier nation that could be picked on by larger countries. We had defeated England on land, thereby gaining our independence, now we had taken powerful France to task on the ocean.

Several years later we again had the opportunity to test the mettle of our navy when the pirates of Tripoli, a country in North Africa, seized our merchant vessels on the Mediterranean Sea and held their crews for ransom. So bold were these outlaws that most of the countries sending ships into that area paid tribute money to them to keep them from molesting their vessels. When some American ships were seized, several of our warships were sent into the Mediterranean to punish the pirates. So successful was our navy in this war that ships flying the American flag went unmolested thereafter by the pirates.

These two conflicts gave our seamen valuable experience. In the first place, it was clearly shown that our ships and men were not only equal to, but superior to most of the ships and men that opposed them. It also taught them many lessons in seamanship which made it possible for them to stand up to any adversary.

Soon after the war with the pirates ended, a new trouble began brewing. England, our old Revolutionary War enemy, began a long series of incidents on the sea which led finally to war. She treated our ships with great disrespect, sometimes stopping them and searching them for "deserters." These attacks were boldly made, often taking place in American waters.

For example, an American ship was entering the New York harbor when a British warship, wishing her to stop to be searched, fired a shot which killed a member of the American crew. Another of our ships had just left Washington, D. C., on its way to the Mediterranean and was still in sight of land when it was attacked by a British warship, and forced to submit to search. Three members of the American ship's crew were killed by gunfire and eighteen were wounded. The British then took four men from the ship, three of them American citizens; the fourth man was hanged as a deserter from the British Navy.

All over America the people were demanding that action be taken against these outrages of the British. When another American vessel was stopped just outside of the New York harbor and a sailor, a citizen of the United States, was taken from it to be forced into service in the British Navy, an American war vessel was ordered to go in search of the British ship to get back the captured seaman. At once the warship left on its task, glad of the opportunity to challenge the British. At dusk one evening it caught up with a British ship which it thought was the guilty one and engaged it in battle. At last the enemy ship gave up and it was only then that the American captain found out that he was not fighting the right ship; instead, his adversary was a powerful twenty-two gun British warship! The important thing was that the American warship won the battle.

No longer could war be avoided. Fighting on land went badly for the Americans and several important battles were lost. However, on the sea, things were different, for our ships were winning victory after victory, much to the surprise of the British. When the war began, they had only contempt for the little American Navy which consisted then of only a dozen or so war vessels while the proud British Navy had more than a thousand warships at her command. What could we do when we were outnumbered almost a hundred to one?

As events turned out, our navy did plenty. Ships were built as rapidly as possible and soon a goodly number of them were on the seas in defiance of the British. Our ship, the **Constitution**, fought and sank the **Guerriere**, and so stoutly did it wage battle that it won for itself the proud title of "Old Ironsides." Today it can still be seen and visited at the Boston Navy Yard.

One of the most memorable battles took place off the coast near

Boston Harbor, between the United States warship **Chesapeake** and the British frigate **Shannon.** In command of the **Chesapeake** was James Lawrence, a famous sea captain.

When Lawrence was only twenty years old he showed great bravery in the war against the Barbary pirates of North Africa and won for himself an enviable reputation as a fighter. When the pirates attacked American merchant vessels, captured their seamen, and demanded ransom money before they would release them, our government decided that the best course of action was to move against them. Other nations were paying tribute to the pirates, but America refused to do so. Instead of sending tribute money to North Africa, we sent warships.

After the pirate fleet had been located, a bold move was proposed. Why not send several small boats in the dark of night among the enemy vessels and set them afire? That way there would be no need to fight the robbers, yet at the same time they would be rendered helpless. No sooner was the plan adopted than it was put into operation.

James Lawrence was one of a small group of American seamen who in seven small boats boldly rowed among the pirate fleet of ships, setting fire to them, one after another. Their task completed, they returned to the safety of their ships, losing only one man in the operation. Later Lawrence was one of five men who disguised themselves as the crew of a ship in distress and requested permission of the pirates to tie their boat to a captured American vessel in the harbor. When their request was granted, they tied to the vessel, boarded it and set it afire, escaping without losing a man, with cannon shot and shell bursting about them.

Because of his bravery and daring, during the War of 1812 he was put in command of the warship **Chesapeake.** It was not a good ship, but was old and out of date though it was heavily armed.

Only a short time after he was given command of the **Chesapeake,** the British warship **Shannon** boldly entered Boston Harbor, challenged the **Chesapeake** to do battle, and withdrew. The **Shannon** was a newer ship than the **Chesapeake** and was superior in many ways to the American vessel, but Lawrence did not hesitate. Like many another American commander of that day, he was confident of victory. The British had long been supreme on the sea, but now the picture was changing. The new navy of the infant United States was giving a wonderful account of itself. Battle after battle was being won. In fact, so superior was our naval fighting force to England's that we were winning by a six to one margin; that is, for every one of our ships destroyed, England was losing six. No wonder our sailors were eager to fight any enemy vessel that it chanced to meet while roaming the high seas. Certainly they would not turn down a challenge.

It was right at this time, when the **Shannon** and the **Chesapeake** met, that England was beginning to feel the real sting of defeat, while the Americans were becoming more bold with every victory. England wanted no more losses; America wanted more victories.

Captain Lawrence sailed his vessel directly into the **Shannon** and each ship raked the other's decks with deadly gunfire. Lawrence was wounded but refused to leave the deck, standing exposed to the shells fired by the furious **Shannon** crew. All about him were death and destruction. The **Chesapeake** was badly wounded and was threatening to sink, but still Lawrence fought on.

Then another shot found its mark and brave Lawrence fell, mortally wounded. As he was carried below he gave his last order to the crew: "Don't give up the ship!"

They did not have to give up the ship that fateful day, for it was so badly shattered and so many of its crew had been killed or wounded that the British simply boarded the **Chesapeake** and claimed it as theirs. There was no one left to deny them the prize.

Captain Lawrence was dead and the British had possession of his ship, but his dying words sped like wildfire from one end of America to the other. Every ship's captain, when he heard the words, took new courage from them and from the courageous example set by the young commander. Captain Perry sailed into battle on Lake Erie only months later with a new flag at his ship's mast; it was blue with bold white letters on it, spelling out Captain Lawrence's last message to his crew: "Don't give up the ship."

More than a century and a half have gone by since that great battle took place in the Atlantic Ocean off the east coast of America, but we still thrill to the words of a dying sailor who could forget his wounds and his fear of approaching death, to give a final courageous order to his ship's crew.

❤

Robert E. Lee

Soldier of a Lost Cause

❤

Almost every visitor to our national capital city of Washington visits Arlington Cemetery, across the Potomac River. Buried there are many of the nation's great leaders. It is a beautiful cemetery, with many paths and trails that wind in and out among the shade trees.

In a prominent spot is the grave of the martyred President, John F. Kennedy, with the eternal flame blowing in the soft breeze. On a rise above his grave are the tombs of our Unknown Soldiers, standing white and silent. In the background is a beautiful Southern mansion, its stately columns standing as they have since the years before the Civil War. This is Arlington, once the home of General Robert E. Lee, now a national shrine.

Seldom has a region revered any man as Robert E. Lee has been honored and loved by the people of the South. Their leader during the desperate and tragic years of the Civil War, he became in defeat their idol. Although a century has passed since he last counseled them in life, the respect of his people has grown rather than diminished with the passing years.

Robert Edward Lee was born on January 19, 1807, into an illustrious family. His father was "Lighthorse Harry" Lee, a distinguished officer of the American Revolution and one-time governor of Virginia. His mother was the brilliant daughter of a wealthy planter, Charles Carter.

Cursed with a life-long mania for gambling and speculation, Robert's father lost his family home and moved to Alexandria, Virginia, across the Potomac from Washington, for there it would be possible to find inexpensive educational facilities for his family. The income at this time consisted of funds from an estate provided by Mrs. Lee's father. Financially things went from bad to worse and when the father died, Robert was left at the age of eleven, with but few resources.

The boy was a quiet and serious student who did well in his studies, being particularly fond of mathematics. His boyhood was quite a normal one and he was fond of outdoor sports, especially horseback riding. After he had completed the local schools, he was faced with the decision of how to continue his education with as little expense involved as possible. His father had always been Robert's idol, and he was proud of the military record that he had made. Now he decided to follow in his father's footsteps and seek a military career. If he could be appointed to West Point, his education would cost him very little and he could be a soldier as his father had been.

The decision made, Robert sought and was granted an appointment to West Point where he proved himself to be an excellent student and a brilliant military strategist. When he graduated, he was next to the top in his class.

For many years his life was typical of that of the military officer of that day. He was gifted with a great natural poise and charm, and the social graces that he learned as a member of a cultured family made him a favorite among his set. He was first assigned to Fort Pulaski, Georgia, where he served for a year and a half; then he next served at Fort Monroe in Virginia for more than three years.

It was while here that he married Mary Ann Randolph Custis, daughter of George Washington Parke Custis, grandson of Martha Washington, the marriage taking place at the family home, "Arlington." He was greatly impressed by the Washington tradition and he sought to be worthy of the ideals of his wife's family as well as those of his own. Seven children were born to the happy marriage that continued for more than forty years.

Lee left Fort Monroe to serve as assistant in the chief engineer's office in Washington, one of his duties while there taking him west of the mountains where he helped to determine the Ohio-Michigan boundary line. He next was assigned to the position of superintending engineer for the St. Louis Harbor and the upper Mississippi and Missouri rivers, where he established an excellent reputation as an efficient engineer. In 1841 he was transferred to a New York Harbor post where he remained for two years.

Lee's next assignment took him to the far West where he saw active duty in the Mexican War, first as an assistant engineer under General Wood, serving at Buena Vista, then transferring to the Vera Cruz scene of operations. There he was given the responsibility for locating the heavy land batteries of the enemy, and his reports proved to be so accurate that they won him the high favor of General Winfield Scott. His work was brilliant wherever he went, at Cerro Gordo, before Mexico City itself, at Churubusco and at the storming of Chapultepec, where he was wounded slightly, rejoining his group the next day. For his gallant conduct he was promoted to the rank of brevet colonel.

With the war's end, he was no longer needed in the West and he was then given the important assignment of building Fort Carroll in Baltimore Harbor, where he remained for almost four years.

In 1852 he was made superintendent of West Point, from which he had graduated twenty-three years earlier. He had not sought the appointment and he was not particularly pleased to accept the post, for he preferred the active life of an officer to that of a "desk general." However, he performed the duties of the post well, making several changes which were recognized as progressive and timely. It was with relief that he relinquished the position three years later to become lieutenant colonel of the 2nd Cavalry in March 1855.

The next several years have been described as a dark period in his life. His wife was afflicted with arthritis and was fast becoming an invalid. Her father died and Lee, as one of the executors of the estate, was forced to spend much time away from his army duties. His long absences from home were particularly unpleasant and for a time he seriously considered resigning from the army, for although his regiment was in Texas, he was in Washington much of the time.

When John Brown's raid at Harper's Ferry occurred in 1859, Lee was in Washington, and he was given the task of putting down the insurrection, which he did, quickly and forcefully. The trouble between the North and the South was becoming more and more heated and talk of secession was heard throught the Southern states. Lee found such talk little to his liking, for both by nature and background he was a loyal patriot. Although he was a true Southerner, he owned no slaves and cared little for the arguments that the people of that region advanced to support their cause.

To Robert E. Lee the issue was a personal one that caused him much sickness at heart. Was his first allegiance to his state or to the Union? Secession was to him revolution, and to take up arms against the Union was treason. Yet, by tradition he was a Virginian, as his family had been for many years before him, and this he could not forget. After much soul-searching, he gave his opinion: If Virginia should secede, he would be forced to cast his lot with her. There could be no other choice for him. He announced his decision while still with his regiment in Texas. He hoped that he would never be called upon to make the choice, but if secession came, that is what it would be.

In Washington the caldron boiled, and preparations for war began. Lee was recalled to the capital city and ordered to "stand by," to await developments. On March 16, 1861, he was given the rank of Colonel of the 1st Cavalry and he accepted the assignment without hesitation. At the same time, the Secretary of War of the Confederate States wrote to him, offering him the rank of Brigadier General in the Confederate States' Army, but he made no reply to this offer. His conscience would not permit him to bear arms against the South, but neither did he want to see the Union dissolved. He realized that now he must accept his full duties as a United States Army man or else resign his post.

The Virginia delegates assembled in convention voted to secede from the Union and Lee therepuon handed in his resignation, effective immediately. He had not been in touch with the Virginia authorities nor had he been consulted by them, so he was still hoping that if war should come, he would not have to take part in it. However, Virginia called upon him to be commander of the state's troops, and he accepted the call three days after he wrote out his resignation from the United States Army. With energy he set about fortifying the rivers and harbors of the state and repulsed a threatened invasion of the state from the west. He was next made assistant to President Jefferson Davis of the Confederate States and sent to organize the defenses along the coast, a task which occupied him until March of the next year, when he was once again summoned back to Richmond. Davis was an extremely difficult man to work with and there were disorganization and jealousies to contend with, but with characteristic patience he bore his burden well.

The Union General McClellan was threatening Richmond, located not far from the Union capital city of Washington, and Lee's task was to defend the city. He was made Commander of the Army of Northern Virginia, and his objective was to keep the army of the North from invading the South and, if possible, to invade the North itself. His troops were inadequate to either task, often being outnumbered two to one. Critics of Lee often disparage his record, but when all factors are considered, including his much smaller forces and his almost constant lack of essential war equipment, his military record cannot be judged harshly.

General McClellan was already pounding at the gates of Richmond; "Stonewall" Jackson was doing his best to fend off three separate Union armies in the Shenandoah Valley to the west; another Union army was coming down the Rappahannock to support McClellan, now only seven miles out of Richmond. Fears were felt everywhere in Virginia that their capital city was doomed; the North was jubilant, for should Richmond fall, a long step toward victory would have been taken.

Instead of waiting to be attacked, Lee took the offensive, and the resulting action, though unsatisfactory in many ways, nevertheless caused McClellan to cease to be an immediate threat to Richmond and relieved for a time the pressure on his forces. Confidence in Lee rose tremendously and the faith that the South had in their leader that later rose to a point of virtual veneration began to make itself felt.

Maneuver followed maneuver, each side seeking an advantage; first one side and then the other gaining momentary superiority. The Union General Pope withdrew to Washington to defend that city, and Lee decided to cross the Potomac River and invade the North. This he did, but miscalculations cost him an advantage on many occasions and the bloody battle of Antietam forced him to withdraw back into Virginia. He had inflicted heavy losses upon his foe, estimated at 27,000, but his own losses, although only half that figure, were nevertheless so heavy that he could not easily take the offensive again until his forces were strengthened. Thus the first invasion of the North resulted in nothing decisive and once again the opposing armies waited in a stalemate, each warily watching the other.

Lee's position was an uncertain one, with food always scarce and supplies inadequate. The winter that followed was particularly bad. With the return of spring came victory for Lee at Chancellorsville, but the accidental shooting of trusted "Stonewall" Jackson by his own troops was a blow to Lee from which he never recovered. Lee was now forced to reorganize his army with a resultant loss of time and cooperative effort.

In spite of this, he decided once again to invade the North, hoping to relieve the pressure on Vicksburg on the Mississippi and also to show the North that their Southern adversary was far from exhausted. He crossed into Maryland, then advanced into Pennsylvania. There at Gettysburg on the first three days of July was fought the war's greatest battle, the losses running to 50,000 men. Neither side won a decisive victory, but Lee's losses were so great that he was sadly forced to withdraw once again across the Potomac into Virginia. From this time on the cause of the South waned. Gettysburg was Lee's greatest defeat. Never would his star rise again to shine as brightly as it did when the battle began on July 1. For the North it was a glorious Fourth of July, for news soon came that Vicksburg had fallen and the Mississippi was once again to flow unvexed to the Gulf of Mexico.

U. S. Grant now took command of the Union forces and vowed to fight it out to a finish. "On to Richmond" became the rallying cry. His army of almost 120,000 men was opposed by Lee's battered force of half that number. Food was so scarce in the territory controlled by Lee's army that rations were reduced to a pint of cornmeal and a bit of bacon for each soldier daily. The fighting became more fierce and intense. In one month's time, Grant lost more than 50,000 men; Lee lost approximately half as many, but it left him with a sadly depleted force. He knew that he could not long continue to take such losses.

Up to this time Lee had been in command of the army of Virginia. Now on February 6, 1865, with defeat almost a certainty, with Northern armies rapidly closing in, he was given the command of all of the Southern armies. Two months later Richmond fell and Lee retreated to Appomattox Courthouse where he surrendered his army to Grant. All that he had left was a pitiable force of less than 8,000 men to surrender their arms to the conquering army. The war was over; the cause of the South was lost.

General Lee was a broken man, without money, without even a country or a home. He was a prisoner of war, though to the credit of the North, he was treated with kindly consideration. His beautiful "Arlington" on the Potomac was lost to him, having been sold for nonpayment of taxes during the war. He accepted the presidency of Washington College and moved to Lexington, Virginia, where he raised the cultural level of the college to new heights. He was under indictment for treason but was never brought to trial.

On those occasions when he journeyed from home he was accorded the highest affection by his countrymen. In peace as in war, he was held in the highest esteem.

He continued to direct the activities of the college until he was stricken on September 28, 1870, dying two weeks later. The entire South was cast into deep gloom. No other man since George Washington was held in such sincere devotion by the people of the South. Washington College was renamed Washington and Lee College in his honor; monuments were erected in his memory; countless eulogies were published praising him. He was both a notable educator and a great soldier. No one since has taken his place in the hearts of his countrymen, for today he stands taller than he ever did at any time during his lifetime though a century has passed since then.

Douglas MacArthur

Five-Star General of the Army

Seldom has a soldier been given the honors that came to General Douglas MacArthur when he was recalled from active duty in Korea by his Commander-in-Chief President. These honors came in part because of victory in the field, but perhaps more because of a recognition of his greatness in personal defeat.

Douglas MacArthur was born on January 26, 1880, into a proud and illustrious family. His father was a soldier and his grandfather a judge. His ancestors were members of the great Campbells of Scotland, of the Clan Artair, from which the name "Arthur" was derived. Back about the year 1250 the Campbells divided into two clans, the MacChaillains and the MacArtairs. The MacArtairs supported Robert Bruce, Scottish king who had been deposed by England, and helped him to win back the throne of Scotland.

In the rough and tumble affairs of the day, the MacArtairs' fortunes declined, and in 1406 their leader, John MacArtair, was beheaded by James I and the clan for a time lost some of its power. However, it continued through the centuries to maintain a strong influence in Scottish affairs, as one of the great clans of the country.

The MacArthurs came to this country during colonial days, settling in Massachusetts where they prospered. Douglas' great-great-grandmother, Sarah Barney Belcher, born during our Revolutionary War in Launton, Massachusetts, was related through various intermarriages, to Franklin D. Roosevelt and Winston Churchill, as well as to Douglas MacArthur.

In the diary of the mayor of Chicapee Falls under the date of June 3, 1845, can still be read this entry: "Mrs. MacArthur had her expected baby last night. It was a boy." The boy was named Arthur and he became the father of Douglas. The house in which he was born still stands, in good repair.

Arthur MacArthur grew up to be an attorney and moved to Milwaukee, Wisconsin, where he entered the Army, seeing service in the Civil War. It was while he was stationed in Little Rock, Arkansas, that a third son was born to Captain and Mrs. MacArthur. They named him Douglas.

As an army captain, the father moved from one army post to another. For a time the family lived on the New Mexican post of Fort Selden, now a crumbling adobe ruin inhabited only by rattlesnakes, roadrunners, and other desert animals. There never was a sense of permanency present, for they all knew that soon they would once again be on the move.

Douglas liked to read and spent many hours a day at his favorite recreation. While he would read almost anything available, he greatly preferred books about wars and military campaigns and became sure as he grew older that the life of a soldier was just about the finest kind of life that anyone could lead. He planned early to attend West Point some day and to prepare for it he enrolled at the West Texas Military Academy for two years, from 1895 to 1897.

There he entered actively in the life of the academy. He was an excellent student, but he spent many hours in athletics also, playing end on the football team, although he was extremely light in weight and was hardly heavy enough to make the team. He enjoyed baseball most of all, however, playing first base and earning a reputation as a good bunter, although generally his hitting was not of the best.

In June 1898, Douglas MacArthur was appointed to the United States Military Academy at West Point but failed to pass the physical examination. The next year he applied again and this time he was accepted. His record there was an excellent one and four years later he graduated with the remarkable grade average of 98.14, the highest average ever attained by any West Point graduate in over a hundred years. Upon his graduation he was commissioned a Second Lieutenant in the Engineers' Corps. Six months later he was promoted to the rank of First Lieutenant.

In 1905, at the age of 25, he had the unusual experience of being assigned as an aide to his father, now a Major General, and the two served together in the Orient.

It was a remarkable coincidence that the son was some day to return to the Philippines, where his father was stationed and there to suffer defeat at the hands of the Japanese, then later to make good the dramatic promise made when driven off the islands by the enemy: "I shall return!"

Returning to America, Douglas MacArthur was next assigned as an aide to President Theodore Roosevelt. He saw action on the Mexican border when bandits under Pancho Villa invaded the American town of Columbus, and was with General Funston's expedition to the Mexican port of Vera Cruz in 1914.

When his illustrious father died in 1912, Douglas MacArthur, now a major, determined to rise as high in military circles as his father had risen. He organized the famous Rainbow Division and as its Chief of Staff, whipped its 27,000 men into such superb condition that it became not only one of the best known, but one of the best all-around divisions in World War I. Before the war ended he was a Brigadier General and was rewarded by having the Distinguished Service Medal conferred upon him. The son had now achieved his goal, for he had risen to a rank equal to that of his father who had one of the most renowned records of any American general to his credit.

General MacArthur was greatly respected by his men. It is true that he was never a popular mixer, but he was, nevertheless, given the admiration that his distinguished record and appearance merited. He was an individualist in many ways, in dress, in speech, and in action. His uniforms were self-designed and often caused comment among his men as well as among the general public. His cap was famous and internationally known; he was seldom without a crop or "stick," especially on formal occasions. Among his men he was known as "The Dude" or sometimes as "The Stick." He was now thirty-eight years old.

During the war, he saw much action and took part in some of the most vicious fighting that took place, on the Marne, at St. Mihiel, at Essey and during the great Meuse-Argonne offensive. Several times he was gassed and twice he was wounded. He was apparently without fear of death and on many occasions he showed it. One time he gave orders that his artillery was to shell the German positions in preparation for an attack and then climbed out of the trenches, with the shells whistling overhead, to observe the effect of the shelling on the German trenches only a few hundred feet away.

He apparently had perfect control over his emotions when under fire. Many soldiers found that they sweat profusely when in dangerous circumstances, but obeservers never knew Douglas MacArthur to sweat under even the most trying conditions. He said one time that he must serve as an example to his men. "They say 'if the old man can take it, I guess I can.'"

Someone has said that MacArthur regarded death "as an experience as uneventful as taking a ride on a Fifth Avenue bus." When a shell hit a farmhouse in which he and his staff were eating, others scattered, but MacArthur never moved from his place. "All Germany," he was quoted as saying, "cannot fabricate the shell that will kill Douglas MacArthur. Sit down with me, gentlemen, sit down." The others shamefacedly did so. Later in Japan when the Japanese were pounding Corregidor, MacArthur was urged to hurry to a nearby shelter. Instead of hurrying, he continued his casual gait with the remark, "The Jap hasn't been born yet who can make me hurry."

One day in Europe a mustard-gas attack took place and MacArthur was badly gassed. He never went about armed, and constantly refused to carry a gas mask, although his soldiers would have been severely disciplined if they had been caught without their masks under similar circumstances. On this day he was almost blinded and it was ten days before the doctors assured him that he would not lose his sight.

When the war ended, it was learned officially just how heavy his losses had been. Of the approximately 40,000 men who had served in the famous Rainbow Division, almost 3,000 had died and another 13,000 had been wounded; eloquent testimonial to their valorous service. Amazingly, only 41 men were listed as having been taken prisoner.

At the war's beginning, Douglas MacArthur had left the United States as a promising young officer, proud of the record that had been made by his famous father. At war's end, he returned, a brigadier general, with a record that matched that of the man who was his idol. As a reward, he was appointed to command West Point, a high honor indeed.

As superintendent of the nation's military academy he sought by every means to make it a better school. Congress wanted to do away with "The Point"; MacArthur saved it. Congress next sought to make it a two-year school; MacArthur opposed the move and won. He changed the curriculum to be more in keeping with the times and insisted upon the highest standards of conduct on the part of the students.

Here too, at West Point, he fell in love with the charming—and wealthy — divorcee, Mrs. Henrietta Brooks, and they were married after a love-at-first-sight meeting at a West Point ball. The wedding took place on St. Valentine's Day, 1922, and was one of the gala affairs of the social season.

In the year 1928 he was sent again to the Philippines, where he had served for several years previously. Two years later he was made a four-star general, an honor that had been awarded to only seven generals previously. He had now surpassed his late father in rank, for the latter had retired with three stars at the age of sixty-four. Douglas MacArthur was now fifty years old.

In 1932 occurred one of the most distasteful affairs of MacArthur's career. He was now Army Chief of Staff and stationed in the nation's capital city. The country was in the midst of a great depression, with millions of people unable to find work. A "bonus march" on Washington took place, about 20,000 men marching on the capitol in an attempt to force Congress to give an immediate cash bonus payment to World War veterans. Congress refused to be coerced, for it was charged—and afterward proved—that the Communists were back of the movement, hoping to bring about trouble between the men and the government.

MacArthur received written orders to disperse the ragtag group and he acted promptly to execute the order with his aide, Dwight D. Eisenhower, by his side as his soldiers drove the squatters out of the city. He was probably the most hated man in America at that moment with the possible exception of Herbert Hoover, president of the United States, the man who gave the order. Some of the men driven out of the city that day had been members of the proud Rainbow Division which he had commanded in France some fifteen years earlier. It was not a task that he relished doing, but the Commander-in-Chief had issued him an order, and like the true soldier that he was, he had obeyed, regardless of personal consequences.

MacArthur was made Chief-of-Staff, and in this capacity he led the inaugural parade of Franklin D. Roosevelt down Pennsylvania Avenue in 1932. When his four-year term was over he returned again to the Philippines to aid in setting up a defense program for that country, for it was widely rumored throughout the Pacific area that Japan was casting longing eyes in that direction. On July 26, 1941, President Roosevelt assigned MacArthur again to active duty as a major general, in command of the U. S. forces in the Far East. War was nearer than they thought, for only four months later the Japanese attacked our naval base in the Hawaiian Islands, Pearl Harbor, and once again we were at war.

Eight hours after Pearl Harbor was attacked, the Japanese launched an attack on the Philippines and MacArthur withdrew to nearby Corregidor to save Manila from being bombed. Now his pitifully small army of 10,000 men was besieged by more than 200,000 Japanese. Their position was hopeless. MacArthur was ordered to go to Australia to avoid capture and to direct the defenses from there. With his family he escaped in a PT boat, vowing, "I shall return!"

The rest of the sad story is history. MacArthur directed the military campaign which had for its purpose the recapture of our lost possessions and the destruction of Japan. Island by island his men moved toward the enemy's homeland, and when at last the Japanese surrendered to save their islands from complete destruction, General Douglas MacArthur was his nation's hero. Perhaps his most triumphant moment occurred when he kept his vow to return to the Philippines.

Wading ashore, he proclaimed, "I have returned. By the grace of Almighty God our forces stand again on Philippine soil."

His only son, now six years old, had known little during his short lifetime but war and destruction. When MacArthur was told that back home in America he had been selected as the "outstanding father of the year," he replied, "My hope is that my son, when I am gone, will remember me not from the battle, but in the home, repeating with him our simple daily prayer, 'Our Father who art in heaven . . .' "

A great honor was now conferred upon him. He was promoted to the highest rank attainable in the Army, General of the Army, with five stars on his collar. It was a fitting reward for the service that he had given his country.

When the war ended, it became MacArthur's task to rebuild Japan, to rid that country of its war faction and to convert it to peaceful ways. The great mass of Japanese people were eager for this new day and for the promise of hope that it held. Their cooperation was excellent and MacArthur did a masterful job of working with them. Seldom has a conqueror earned greater respect from the people conquered than he did from the Japanese. He administered justice with a firm hand, restored freedom of speech and of the press, freed political prisoners and jailed war criminals, elevated the Japanese women to a position of respect in both the home and in society, and in short, rebuilt Japan upon new, democratic lines. For five years he was that country's virtual ruler and he earned a real place in the affections of everyone.

War again broke out in the Orient when the Republic of Korea was attacked by the Communist North Koreans in 1950, and at once General MacArthur was directed by the President to resist the invading forces, later being named United Nations Commander. The work of driving out the invading North Koreans was going well when MacArthur, accused of exceeding his authority and of not cooperating with the Commander-in-Chief, was suddenly removed from command and he returned to civilian life, hurt and disappointed.

He now returned to the United States where he was everywhere given a hero's welcome. On April 19, 1951, he addressed a joint session of Congress where he was given a tremendous ovation. On radio and television, the occasion was viewed and heard by millions of fellow Americans. His military career was ended. Now, he said, he would "just fade away, an old soldier who tried to do his duty as God gave him the light to see that duty."

In New York City, where he now chose to live with his wife and son, the welcoming parades and receptions did full honor to his achievements and demonstrated his popularity with the people. They enjoyed their new life to the utmost and entered into the festivities with obvious relish. Here they lived until, on April 4, 1964, General MacArthur died at the age of eighty-four. The magnificence of his funeral services, viewed by millions on television, was a last testimonial to a fine gentleman and a great soldier.

Oliver Hazard Perry

"We Have Met the Enemy and They Are Ours"

The War of 1812 has sometimes been called America's second "war of independence" because it was fought to show both England and France that they would have to treat us as a free and independent nation, which neither of those two countries was doing. France was just as guilty as England was, but since Britain was "mistress of the seas" by virtue of her much larger navy, it was natural that she would commit many more offenses on the sea than France would with her fewer ships.

Protests by the American Government went unheeded until finally in desperation our government declared war on England on June 18, 1812. As a nation we were grossly unprepared for war. Some of the people thought that we should go to war, but many did not. The New England states knew that their shipping would suffer if war was declared, and so that part of the country resisted the war efforts, even going so far as to suggest that the Union be dissolved, with the New England states seceding and forming a separate country.

In Congress there was also a sharp division of opinion, 49 representatives voting against war and 79 voting in favor of it. In the Senate, the vote was even closer, 19 to 13. However, once war was declared, efforts began to be made to wage it and plans were formulated.

One of the major objectives of the war was the conquest of Canada, a task which our forces were quite sure would not be a formidable one, but as events turned out, this was an opinion that proved to be very wrong.

Along the border lakes was a series of Canadian defenses, from upper Lake Michigan to Lake Champlain. The plan was to take these forts and so expose all of Canada to possible conquest. It was essentially a plan that would have worked provided we had more capable commanders who had learned to work together. As it was, we lacked men of experience and ability in the army and their efforts were signally unsuccessful.

For example, General Hull, who commanded the American forces at Detroit, proved to be not only a very poor general, but a coward as well. With 2,500 men under his command he could well have resisted almost any force that the British could put in the field against him. However, when he crossed into Canada and met the British General Brock, who commanded a force only half as strong as Hull's—half of them untrained Indians—he turned about and fled back to Detroit.

General Brock, surprised at Hull's retreat, followed him to Detroit and surrounded the fort with his inferior forces and demanded its surrender. To his further surprise, Hull at once, without firing a shot, turned Detroit over to Brock, thus opening the frontier to Indian raids and creating discouragement in the American army at a time when there should have been vigor and enthusiasm.

Other border efforts were equally unsuccessful. The soldiers sent to capture Montreal marched as far as the Canadian line but refused to go further and they promptly were marched back home again by their commander. An army from Niagara invaded Canada but was easily repulsed and its commander was removed in disgrace.

At the River Raisen, in the West, the Americans were defeated and forced to surrender. On the night of their victory, the Indians, crazed by liquor, fell upon the American wounded, who had been left unguarded, and killed them to a man. "Remember the Raisen!" became the battle cry of the now infuriated American soldiers.

Then a new ray of hope appeared and was seized upon with vigor. The Americans knew that as long as the British held control of Lake Erie, Detroit could never be recaptured, for it could be supplied indefinitely by boats. It was apparent that the first step would have to be the clear control of Lake Erie by American forces. Then Detroit could be recaptured and the territory around it made safe once again for the Americans.

The man selected to clear the lake of the enemy was Oliver Hazard Perry, a young officer of the United States Navy. Upon him rested the hopes of a nation.

Oliver Perry was born in the little village of Rocky Brook, Rhode Island, on August 20, 1785, and at the time the assignment was given to him to regain control of Lake Erie he was only twenty-seven years old. Yet so confident were his superiors in his ability to do what everyone knew was so vitally important, that there was no hesitation on their part to give him the assignment.

He attended the elementary school in Rocky Brook, after which he went to Newport to study navigation there, having indicated a strong interest in going to sea. At the age of fourteen he was appointed midshipman on his father's ship, the **General Greene,** and on it saw active service in the West Indies during our naval war with France. Later during our war with the pirates along the Barbary Coast in the Mediterranean Sea he was on duty there, serving on several war vessels.

He was only eighteen years old when he was given the rank of Acting Lieutenant and four years later was granted a permanent lieutenantcy. He was then assigned the task of building gunboats in Rhode Island and Connecticut, later being put in command of these boats to enforce the shipping embargo then in effect. The next year he was made master of the schooner **Revenge** which saw active service in the Atlantic in the naval action against Great Britain which led to the War of 1812.

Since he was anxious to be at the scene of the greatest possible action, in February 1813, he was sent to Sackett's Harbor on Lake

Erie under Commodore Isaac Saunders, who put him in command of the naval forces on Lake Erie. Now he clearly saw his responsibility to build a fleet capable of clearing the British from Lake Erie, who now were in complete control of that large body of water. It was the British vessels which were supplying Detroit, and Perry knew that as long as this went on, Detroit could not be returned to American hands.

The task that he faced was an enormous one. To build the fleet alone presented difficulties almost impossible to overcome, for the lumber to be used had to be cut from the trees in the region and it would of necessity be green and hard to work with. However, he set to work, and from the wilderness forest a little fleet gradually emerged. Within four months he could proudly say that the first part of his mission had been accomplished, for ten vessels of war floated in the Erie waters off the town of the same name. True, they were small ships, the largest being of only 480 tons, which he named the **Lawrence** after Captain James Lawrence, who only a short time before had given his life in a battle with the British off Boston, but who had left to the world his dying words, "Don't give up the ship!"

The task of equipping his vessels with guns, supplies, and men was almost as arduous a job as that of building them. However, this too was accomplished in time, and the fleet prepared for the mission for which it had been built: to seek out the enemy and destroy them. To get out into the open lake the guns and equipment of the heaviest vessels had to be removed, for the water was so shallow that some of his ships could not otherwise get over the sand bar that lay between the shore and the main water of the lake.

For some unexplained reason, the enemy vessels which had lain off shore for some time did not challenge Perry and his fleet as they emerged, but instead sailed westward and took up a position on the Detroit River with the obvious intention of protecting the city from the newly built fleet. Perry and his ships followed the enemy, dropping anchor in Put-in-Bay, about twenty miles north of the present city of Sandusky, from where he could keep watch on the enemy and also be in close contact with General William Henry Harrison to the south, whose later victorious campaign was one day to make him President of the United States.

The time had come for action, Perry decided. First he sailed close to the British to take count of their strength and found that they had been strengthened by a new ship, the **Detroit,** which the British Commander, Robert Barclay, made his flagship. In addition, Barclay had the vessel **Queen Charlotte** and four smaller ships under his command. Against these six vessels Perry's ten were pitted. Perry decided that the chances of victory were good and he was eager to match strength with the enemy.

Commodore Barclay, emboldened by the addition of the **Detroit** to his fleet and by the necessity of securing needed supplies, decided that a contest with Perry for the possession of the lake must now take place. At dawn on the morning of September 10, Barclay's fleet sailed out of its place of refuge onto Lake Erie and was promptly sighted by Perry's lookout. At once Perry gave the order to weigh anchor, and his vessels sailed out of the harbor to challenge the enemy.

A plan of battle was made before the fight began. Perry's ship, the **Lawrence,** was to oppose the flagship **Detroit;** the **Niagara** was to contest the British **Queen Charlotte;** his smaller vessels were to take on the smaller vessels of the enemy. It was ten o'clock in the morning when Perry raised on his flagship a banner on which were sewed the words: "Don't Give Up the Ship!" The decks were cleared for action. All was in readiness for the battle which both commanders knew would decide the fate of the region.

It was noon before the battle began, lacking fifteen minutes. The **Lawrence** sailed boldly toward the **Detroit** and opened fire. For some time these two vessels were the only ones engaged and it soon became apparent that the issue that day would be decided by the two flagships. The battle waged for three hours. When the **Lawrence** was so battered that it could no longer stay afloat, with all her guns out of commission and eighty-three of her crew of a hundred and three either dead or wounded, Perry took his battle flag and, amid shot and shell, rowed to the **Niagara,** at once bringing that vessel into action against the enemy. The issue was now decided quickly; in a few minutes the British ships struck their colors and the battle was over.

Commander Barclay himself was dead, as were forty-four of his men, and ninety-four more were wounded. Perry's losses included twenty-seven dead and ninety-six wounded. Of these casualties, more than two thirds were members of the **Lawrence's** crew. It was as fierce a battle as had been fought when Captain Lawrence himself fell in his ship's engagement with the British.

The plan of the Americans had worked well. Now General Harrison moved against Detroit, and with the water route blocked, the garrison had no choice but to surrender. The area about it was once again in the hands of the Americans. No longer would settler's homes be burned by the savages or their families be carried off into captivity. The frontier was safe once more.

Perry was given full credit for the victory, which was due to a large extent, to his bravery and determination to win. To his commanding officer, General Harrison, he sent a message that has been remembered by Americans ever since: "We have met the enemy and they are ours." Thus was the story of the battle told in just a few words.

To the United States Secretary of the Navy, he sent these words, "It has pleased the Almighty to give to the arms of the United States a signal victory over their enemies on this lake."

When the news was received in Washington, President Madison immediately promoted Perry to the rank of captain. No honor was too great to confer upon the new hero. To the prize money of $7,500, which was his, Congress added another $5,000. That body also passed a resolution thanking him for the victory and requested that a gold medal be struck to be given to him. Several state legislatures voted him their thanks. Cities gave him gifts and held receptions in his honor. No British fleet had ever before been captured by the American navy, so it was small wonder that the joy of the nation was so great.

Captain Perry's life after his famous victory continued to be an adventurous one. In command of a new ship, the **Java,** carrying forty-four guns, he cruised the Mediterranean. At one time he was challenged to a duel, but although his adversary shot at him, Perry did not fire his gun.

In May 1819, he was put in command of a number of vessels and sent to South America where ships of several of the countries had been preying on American merchant vessels. While sailing on the broad waters of the Orinoco River in Venezuela, he fell ill with the dread yellow fever, then the scourge of the tropics, and after a few days of suffering, he died, only three days after his thirty-third birthday.

Perry was buried at Port of Spain on the island of Trinidad, though several years later his body was brought back to America, to its final resting place at Newport. There his home state of Rhode Island, proud of its hero, erected a granite monument to his memory. His most enduring monument, however, were the words that he sent to his superior officer after the battle on Lake Erie: "We have met the enemy and they are ours!"

George Washington
"Father of His Country"

Have you ever wondered why George Washington came to be known as the "Father of His Country"? Surely such an honor would not be given to any man unless he had done more for his country than perhaps any other person had done. Because the American people have felt that there probably would be no United States of America today if it had not been for General Washington, to him has been given the honor of being called his country's father.

When George was a boy, he learned the ways and manners that made him loved and respected as a man. His family knew him to be dependable, honest, and truthful, and willing to do the things that were expected of him. He was quiet and shy, but he loved games and sports. He was especially fond of horseback riding and since he lived on a large farm, called a "plantation," he had plenty of opportunities to ride, sometimes for hours at a time. Since there were many woods on the farm, he also hunted, and he liked to roam the forests in search of game. Swimming was also a favorite sport of his. These out-of-door activities made him strong and rugged, and since he was a tall man, well over six feet in height, he was an imposing figure, especially on horseback. Because of his quiet, sure ways and his confidence in himself, he commanded the respect of all who knew him.

He had an older half brother, Lawrence, who was very fond of him, and when their father died, Lawrence asked George to come and live with him at Mount Vernon on the banks of the Potomac River in Virginia. Lawrence gave George all of the affection and attention that his father would have given him, and although George did not attend a school such as we have today, he was given tutoring by teachers who came to Mount Vernon to instruct him.

One of his neighbors was Lord Fairfax, who hired him to survey some lands in the wilderness to the west. George Washington did such a good job of surveying the wild lands that he was given the position of public surveyor. Now he spent many days in the unsettled forests, and his knowledge of life in the wilderness was as great as that of any man of his time.

When war broke out between France and England, the British general, Braddock, was sent into what is now western Pennsylvania to seize Fort Pitt (now the city of Pittsburgh), then held by the French. When General Braddock and his men were almost to Fort Pitt, they were ambushed by an army of French and Indians, and General Braddock was killed. George Washington quickly took command and because of his knowledge of Indian ways, he saved the British army from destruction. Now the people knew that they had a good leader in their midst and Washington was made commander of the state of Virginia troops, a position that he held for three years.

Washington longed for the pleasant life of a plantation owner, and in the year 1759 he returned to Mount Vernon, which he now owned, as Lawrence had died and left the large plantation to him. Here he spent the next six years of his life, overseeing the work of the farm, and taking care of the many details that were so necessary if the farm was to be run well. Washington was never satisfied unless it was managed in the best manner possible. He would have been happy to spend the rest of his life here, but fate was not to permit him to live a pleasant life of ease.

All of the American colonies, including Virginia, were owned by England at that time, and trouble had broken out between the mother country and her colonies. This trouble became so severe that the leaders met in Philadelphia to decide what should be done. George Washington, dressed in his best military uniform, was a member of the Congress, and because the men from the other colonies remembered his bravery in the wilderness campaign several years before, they elected him Comander-in-Chief of the Continental Army. This was in June 1775.

Washington did not know what to do. Should he accept the honor that his fellow countrymen had offered to him? If he did, it would mean that he could no longer live at his beloved Mount Vernon, but that he would have to live the rough life of a soldier, moving from camp to camp. What if he should be killed in battle? Or what would happen if the colonists should lose their struggle for freedom? He might well be imprisoned or even shot; perhaps Mount Vernon would be taken from him and given to some loyal subject of the king. All of these thoughts came to George Washington as he sought to reach a decision.

However, he did not hesitate long. Their mother country was unjust to them, he believed; his fellow men trusted him and wanted him as their leader. Surely he was not afraid to do what his conscience told him that he must do. He would be their leader; he would give them victory; yes, he would be their new commander-in-chief.

At Cambridge, just outside of Boston, in Massachusetts, he took command of the newly created American army. It was not much of an army, he had to admit. Most of the men were untrained; other generals were jealous of him and did not work well with him. Food, clothing, and military supplies were scarce, for the governments of the thirteeen colonies that made up the little struggling nation did not work together, and sometimes even refused to provide their share of desperately needed supplies and equipment. Sometimes the outlook was so black that General Washington wondered if they could ever win their independence.

Many of his soldiers, long unpaid, dressed in rags, sometimes without shoes during cold winter months, lost heart and deserted, returning to their homes and families. Why should they suffer as they did, risking their lives for a country that did not appreciate them? Thus they reasoned, and not finding a satisfactory answer in their own minds, they left camp and returned home, often hundreds of miles away.

However, after seven long years, final victory came at York-town in Virginia when the British general, Cornwallis, surrendered to Washington. Now America was free and George Washington could again return to the life that he liked best, that of a gentleman farmer at Mount Vernon. Gladly he gave up his command, though it was with sorrow that he said good-bye to the soldiers who had followed him through so many battles.

In the year 1781 he returned to Mount Vernon and was once more happy in his role as a farmer. However, all did not go well in the new nation. A colony did not always trust a neighboring colony; the government of the country was weak and it could not enforce the laws that it made or collect the tax money that it needed so badly. Finally a new convention was called and the Constitution of the United States of America was written and adopted. Washington was elected to be the first president in the year 1789. Once again he left Mount Vernon, this time to be gone for eight years, for he was re-elected to serve a second four-year term in 1793. So it wasn't until 1798 that he again said farewell to his co-workers and retired once more to Mount Vernon.

Though Washington desired nothing more than to live at peace with the world at Mount Vernon, he was once more asked to give up his life as a gentleman farmer to serve as commander-in-chief of our armed forces. Trouble with France developed over a series of incidents, and when the government of that country demanded that we pay them a large sum of money as tribute, feeling ran high in America and preparations for war began. The building of a navy began, and George Washington was called upon to again head our army. However, the trouble blew over and Washington gratefully returned home.

Philadelphia had served as our national capital for several years; then the seat of our central government was moved to New York City. It was here that Washington was inaugurated first President of the United States in 1789. The next year, the central government was once again returned to Philadelphia with the understanding that it was to remain there for ten years. During this time a new capital city was to be hewn out of the wilderness on both sides of the Potomac River, part of the city to be on the Maryland side and part on the Virginia side. In honor of our first president, the new city was to be called Washington and the region about it was to be known as the District of Columbia. The location was close to Washington's home, and he watched with great interest the beginnings of the new city.

George Washington died before the federal government moved from Philadelphia to its new location on the Potomac, but he lived long enough to know that a beautiful city was arising near his plantation that would some day make America proud of it.

In the summer of the year 1800, only months after George Washington's death, the city of Washington became our nation's capital. It was a sorry pioneer city when the new president, John Adams, moved into his new home, known today as the White House. The Capitol, too, was unfinished, and few of the public buildings were ready for their occupants. The streets were only trails through the woods and were so muddy that even horses could hardly go down them. In the East Room of the White House where today the President's grand receptions are held, the President's wife hung the family wash.

Many government officials were afraid to live in Washington at that time because they feared that the hot, moist climate was bad for their health. It was many years before the city began to take on the beautiful appearance that makes it today one of the world's best planned capital cities.

When Washington retired from active life he was almost sixty-eight years of age, though he still loved to supervise the many daily activities of his plantation. One cold and rainy day in December of the year 1799, he spent many hours on horseback, inspecting his broad fields. He returned home, tired and chilled. A severe cold developed which quickly became worse. After a few days of suffering, he died, his long and busy life ended. He was buried near his home where today his body lies in a tomb next to that of his wife.

Today Mount Vernon is a national shrine, visited by thousands of people who come to pay their respects to the man who became known as the "Father of His Country." It was said of him that he was "First in war, first in peace, and first in the hearts of his countrymen."

Ulysses Simpson Grant

From Store Clerk to the White House

Few Presidents have risen from the ranks faster than Ulysses S. Grant. At the age of thirty-eight he was clerking in his father's hardware and leather goods store, trying, not too successfully, to earn enough money to support his family. Eight years later he was elected President of the United States.

One may well believe that any man with a record such as that must have been a very unusual person and have led an interesting life. This certainly was true of Ulysses S. Grant.

He was born in Mount Pleasant in the state of Ohio in the year 1822. His parents were quite ordinary small-town people who had little more than enough means to enable them to live comfortably. His father was a farmer and also a leatherworker, and young Ulysses (he was for some reason called "Sam" by his friends) helped his father with his daily work. He did not like leatherworking, though he did enjoy living on a farm. He was especially fond of horses, as most boys were in those days, and it was said that he often drove a team about the farm doing various chores when he was only seven or eight years old.

On one occasion there was much wood to be hauled to the village home from a place about a mile in the country and young Ulysses drove the team back and forth, making many trips, until there was enough wood stored up to last through the winter. While he was much too small to load and unload the wood, he was able to drive the team without any trouble, and in so doing, did the work of a man.

He did much other work about the farm, too. Of course, there was plowing to be done, and later on "dragging" and disking and cultivating the soil. When the crops were mature, there was harvesting to be done, grain to be stored, and hay to be cut and gathered and stored in the barn. In those days, the homes and most small-town business places were heated by stoves that burned wood, and since there were no gasoline engines then to turn the saws to cut the wood, all of the fuel had to be cut by hand. Naturally, Ulysses did his full share of woodcutting and sawing, as did the other members of the family.

However, life on the farm was not all work and no play. In the summer he went fishing in the brook that flowed through the farm, and in one place where the water was a little deeper than it was in most places, the boys had a "swimming hole" where they spent many pleasant hours during the hot summer months. In the wintertime the creek froze over and then the boys put on their skates and went up and down the frozen stream. Ulysses liked to drive the horses then, too, when the ground was covered with snow, and he, sitting in a small sled which was called a "cutter" and all bundled up to protect him against the cold wind, would drive through the white countryside, the horses pulling him briskly over the icy roads.

Because he liked horses and spent much time with them, he became an expert horseman and a very skillful rider.

Ulysses did not care much for school and was not an especially good scholar, although his father did his best to encourage the boy to apply himself. When he was old enough he applied for admission to West Point and was accepted. The old habits that he had made at home continued at the military academy and his studies were often neglected. However, his horsemanship was excellent and he was highly regarded as a rider. At the end of four years he graduated, but his record was only average and he ranked twenty-first in a class of thirty-nine.

About the time that he finished West Point, the Mexican War began and Ulysses Grant was sent to that scene of action where he served well and honorably and earned for himself an enviable reputation for being a brave and fearless man. On several occasions it was felt that he took needless chances and his men often feared for his life, but he survived the war, deciding to remain in the Army at least for the time being. However, he married and, after several years, resigned from the Army, once again taking up farming as a means of earning a living. He found this work too exhausting, however, and for reasons of health gave up farming and went into the real estate business, buying and selling land and houses. While this work was more to his liking, it did not pay enough for him to support his family on his earnings and he finally accepted his father's offer to become a clerk in his hardware and leather goods store. Here he remained for some time, and here he was working at the time that the war broke out between the states in 1860.

Abraham Lincoln had been elected President, and the South, fearful that he was about to free the slaves, decided to leave the Union and form a country of their own, which they called the Confederate States of America. Lincoln had taken an oath when he became President to preserve the Union, and this he determined to do, even though it might result in warfare between the states. When Fort Sumter was fired upon by the Confederates in the harbor at Charleston, South Carolina, actual fighting began that was not to end until four years of very bloody conflict had gone by.

With the war's beginning, Ulysses Grant, now thirty-eight years of age, suddenly seemed to find his true calling. He enlisted in the army and helped to organize troops that were being made ready to take part in the fighting. His West Point training and his Mexican War record were both to his advantage and he was made a colonel, then quickly advanced to the rank of brigadier general. The slowness of purpose, the apathy, the lack of decision that had marked his life heretofore were now gone and he became a capable and zealous officer.

Extending through Kentucky and Tennessee, from the Mississippi River to the Appalachian Mountains, were several Confederate forts, forming what they considered to be their first line of defense. Two of their most important forts were Fort Donelson and Fort Henry. These Grant and his troops captured, over 15,000 Confederate troops surrendering at Fort Donelson alone. With these two strongholds in the hands of the Union troops, the Confederates were forced to give up the important cities of Nashville and Columbus and retreat southward to what they called their second line of defense.

As they fled, General Grant and his men pursued them, allowing them no rest. At Pittsburg Landing in Tennessee the two armies met, and after two days of furious fighting with heavy losses on both sides, Grant was at last able to drive the enemy from the field and claim a great victory. Things looked black indeed for the Confederates, for now they had to yield still further and give up their second line of defense. Grant wished to gain control of the entire Mississippi River, for in so doing he would literally cut the South in two, separating Texas and adjoining states from the Eastern states, and it would then be possible for the great and productive Midwest region to once again ship its products south to the Gulf of Mexico and thence to the Atlantic Ocean.

The Confederates now had only two major strongholds left on the Mississippi River, Vicksburg and Port Hudson, and these Grant determined to capture next. After heavy fighting, he succeeded in laying siege to Vicksburg. For seven long weeks that city held out, suffering terribly from hunger and disease. At last the brave and determined defenders were forced to surrender, for they were starving, having eaten even the rats and mice of their city in their efforts to stave off capture by the enemy.

On the fourth of July, 1863, the day after the Confederate general met defeat at Gettysburg in the greatest battle of the war, Vicksburg surrendered its garrison of 32,000 men. Four days later Port Hudson surrendered and the great Father of Waters was again in Union hands, from its beginning in the far-north state of Minnesota to the delta of the river in the Gulf of Mexico. It was the beginning of the end for the Confederacy.

General Grant's brilliant record in the West was recognized by President Lincoln, who had much reason to be displeased with many of his generals in the eastern theater of war, and Grant was made commander-in-chief of all the Union armies. He now went east and took command of the armies that were fighting Confederate General Robert E. Lee in Virginia. In a message to the President, General Grant said, "I propose to fight it out on this line if it takes all summer."

It did take all summer, and his losses were terrific, tens of thousands of men being lost in the fighting, but Grant never gave up and never yielded an inch of ground. The final outcome was inevitable and finally Lee could hold out no longer. At Appomattox Courthouse in Virginia, Generals Grant and Lee met on a Sunday morning and there the Confederate general surrendered what was left of his once magnificent army to Grant.

General U. S. Grant was as forgiving in peace as he had been relentless in war. When he was asked by General Lee what was to be done with the horses and mules of his soldiers, Grant replied, "Let them take them home with them. They will need them for the spring plowing."

Grant was now America's hero. No honor was too great to bestow on him. A quiet, modest man, he was often ill at ease in large gatherings and at affairs of state. However, his fame had been established, and when a candidate was needed for the presidency in 1868, Grant was nominated, and in the November election he was chosen by the people of the country that he had helped to save to be their leader for the next four years. When his first term was over, he was re-elected for another term.

He was happy when it came time to leave the White House for he often confessed that he had never felt quite at home there. Now he decided to take a trip around the world. His fame had gone before him and wherever he went, he was welcomed with the greatest honor and enthusiasm.

After he returned home, he lived quietly, spending much of his time writing the interesting story of his life. He suffered financial reverses and determined to pay off all his debts, though legally he would not have had to. He was stricken with cancer and it became a race with death to see if he could finish his memoirs before he died. This he was able to do, and he died at peace, knowing that his creditors would be paid off in full.

He died on July 23, 1885, and the tomb that marks his grave on the banks of the Hudson River in New York City is a fitting testimonial to a great man and a fine soldier.

Index